P9-DND-549

The
girlfriends
Keepsake Book

Copyright © 1996 Carmen Renee Berry and Tamara C. Traeder

Cover Image: *Entre Nous* by Willabel Cole Mitchell. Reproduced with permission of Jean Duggan.

Photograph in "Now We Can Look Back and Laugh" reproduced with permission of Jeanie Jensen. Copyright © 1971 Jeanie Jensen.

Remaining photographs reproduced with permission of Kalen Meyer. Copyright © 1996 Kalen Meyer. Photo transfers of all photographs by Kalen Meyer.

"Swimming, for Marilyn" by Carolyn Miller was first published in full in *Zone 3*, Spring 1991. Excerpt reproduced with permission of Carolyn Miller.

All Rights Reserved under International and Pan-American Copyright Conventions. Published in the United States by Wildcat Canyon Press, a division of Circulus Publishing Group, Inc. No part of this book may be reproduced in whole or in part without written permission from the publisher, except by a reviewer who may quote brief passages in a review; nor may any part of this book be reproduced, stored in a retrieval system, or transmitted in any form or by any means electronic, mechanical, photocopying, recording, or other without written permission from the publisher.

Publisher: Julienne Bennett
Senior Editor: Roy M. Carlisle
Copyeditor: Priscilla Stuckey
Cover and Interior Design: Dana Nakagawa, Gordon Chun Design

Printed in Canada

For a catalog of our publications please write:

Wildcat Canyon Press
2716 Ninth Street, Berkeley, CA 94710
Phone (510) 848-3600 Fax (510) 848-1326
Email Circulus@aol.com

Library of Congress Cataloging-in-Publication Data

Berry, Carmen Renee.
    The girlfriends keepsake book: the story of our friendship / Carmen Renee Berry and Tamara Traeder.
    p. cm.
ISBN 1–885171–13–7 (hardcover)
    1. Female friendship. 2. Women—Psychology. I. Traeder, Tamara, 1960–   . II. Title.
BF575.F66B45 1996
302.3'4'082—dc20   96—29374 CIP

Distributed to the trade by Publishers Group West
10 9 8 7 6 5 4 3

The
girlfriends
Keepsake Book

The Story of Our Friendship

Carmen Renee Berry
and
Tamara Traeder

WILDCAT CANYON PRESS

A Division of Circulus Publishing Group, Inc.

Berkeley, California

A Story to Tell

What would we do without our girlfriends? Are they not amazing women? If you are fortunate, you have a friend who is there when you need her, who can put matters into perspective or make you laugh, and who knows your worst mistakes and most unsavory fears about yourself and loves you anyway. She is the person with whom you can sit comfortably in silence, and yet the same individual to whom you have so much to say. A girlfriend can sometimes see your situation more clearly than you can, and you can trust her to tell you what she really thinks is the best course for you. And even though all friends have disagreements—silent or acknowledged—these relationships seem surprisingly easy.

These seemingly miraculous relationships, however, frequently go unheralded and unrecorded. Our modern society has never set much store by women's friendships, frequently dismissing them as shallow institutions, chiefly there to facilitate shopping expeditions and restroom visits. But the lucky women who have experienced the trust level and support that is available in female friendship know better. As women have started honoring themselves and others as women, we have come to realize the essential role that women friends play in each other's lives. Some of these true characteristics have been revealed in movies such as *Fried Green Tomatoes*, *The Color Purple*, *Waiting to Exhale*, and *How to Make an American Quilt*. These accounts offer up honesty, acceptance, loyalty, laughter—the gifts that the bonds of friendship can offer women friends.

We have very much enjoyed witnessing the themes of friendship in these fictional characters. However, we also wanted to hear some true stories about friendships among women. When we were interviewing women about their friendships for the book *girlfriends: Invisible Bonds, Enduring Ties*, we were touched and surprised by the variety and richness of the stories women had to tell.

Additionally, after the book was released, we heard hundreds more anecdotes and rituals of friendship from women. Women were eager to share their stories about their friends. What became increasingly clear to us was that every woman and her closest friend or friends had a story (or many stories) to tell. This book will allow you to record those stories—your history, your future plans—together. We think every friendship is valuable and worth recording. We hope that this book will provide you with an opportunity to do so.

A note about writing your memories, plans, and wishes in this book: No story is written in one sitting, and frequently it is rewritten, added to, reexamined. This story of your friendship does not need to be written all at once. Record as you go along, and fill the spaces as the muse strikes you. If you do not have anything to say on a page, do not feel obligated to fill the space. There will be experiences in the future or other memories that will come to you that you will want to record.

We have often said that we are looking forward to old age and collecting more tales of adventure with our women friends. After all, these are the women who have shaped us. By recording our history together, we are recording our development as people. So we encourage you to save some spaces for adding new memories and stories and wishes. You and your women friends have the rest of your lives to make history together!

This book is dedicated to the
friendship that is shared by

....

and

....

Part of Our History

Authentic female friendship is when
we allow another woman
to see our core, go to our core,
and risk sharing our souls.

—SUE MONK KIDD

Before Our Friendship Began

I was born on _____.

The president in office when I was born was _____.

I lived in _____ on _____.
CITY   STREET

I went to school at _____.
SCHOOL

The most notable thing about my appearance on this planet was:

_____

_____

THIS IS WHAT I LOOKED LIKE:
(Paste baby pictures here)

You were born on _____.

The president in office when you were born was _____.

You lived in _____ on _____.
CITY   STREET

You went to school at _____.
SCHOOL

The most notable thing about your appearance on this planet was:

_____

_____

THIS IS WHAT YOU LOOKED LIKE:

(Paste baby pictures here)

Little did we know then, but in _____ we would meet and become girlfriends!
YEAR

Who Was That Woman Anyway?

We are meeting women all the time. Sometimes we recall exactly the moment we met a friend. Sometimes it takes a while after we've met before we really notice her. But there comes a moment when she stands out from other people, when we experience a yearning to get to know her better. See if you can remember that time when you first noticed your friend to be.

I first noticed you when . . .

You meet your friend, your face brightens — you have struck gold. — KASSIA

JEANNE AND NANCY IMMEDIATELY WERE DRAWN TOGETHER when they met.
As Jeanne tells the story: "I had gone to a party with a man I was dating at the
time, and I met Nancy in the backyard of the house in which the party was being
held. I was first so attracted to her because of her eyes — I thought she had the
most beautiful green eyes. It was so odd because I felt this immediate sense of
closeness to her, and I later found she felt the same way about me. As we talked,
we discovered many similarities in our lives — we are both from the Midwest, we
both lost a parent at an early age, we both enjoy the same outdoor activities such as
canoeing and hiking. On the surface, I don't think anyone would think we would
be so attracted to each other — she is shy and somewhat introverted, and I am more
aggressive and outgoing. But somehow we recognized each other at a level that I
do not believe was conscious. We knew right away we would be good, good friends.
Today, five years later, she is one of the most important people in my life."

I Knew We Would Be Friends

At the first meeting, some women know they are going to be friends; an instant connection makes them feel they have known each other forever. Other times friendship takes more time to develop; one or both women may not have seen each other's qualities right away. The beauty of friendship is that it can have its own pace; it need not be rushed and pressured. We would like you to record your first memories of your friendship. When did you know you were going to be friends with each other?

ELIZABETH AND JOYCE BOTH ATTENDED A MEETING for volunteers at a hospice. This was the first time at the hospice for both of them, but each got the impression that the other had been there a long time and was more qualified for the work. Then Elizabeth mentioned her ex-husband named Fred, and Joyce took note, as she was in the process of leaving *her* husband, Fred. After the meeting, they introduced themselves, realized that they were each feeling intimidated by the other one, and then started trading stories of ex-husbands named Fred. That got them to lunch, and as Joyce notes, "We haven't stopped eating together since then!"

One of the characteristics that I found
so appealing about you was . . .

I knew we'd be friends when . . .

One of my first memories of our friendship is . . .

Our Friendship Has Made Me a Better Person

We learn various lessons from our friends as we grow older, especially what they teach by example. Through their actions and attitudes, they help us learn to navigate life's problems and confront our personal demons. Watching how a friend resolves a tense situation at work or uses her anger positively in a social situation helps us learn to find positive and mature ways to live. Likewise, you may have learned how to confront a difficult family issue and can provide an example for her. In either case, we help one another become more mature and stronger women. As Catherine, a woman we interviewed, said, "My friends have given me life. They have helped me create myself." Can you think of a way that your friendship has made you a better person?

Our friendship has made me a better person (don't you agree?). From you I've learned . . .

HELEN, SIXTY-FOUR, SUMS UP THE EFFECT HER FRIENDSHIPS have had on her: "I realize more than ever how the person I am at this moment is a composite of the friends who have shaped me by their presence in my life. I treasure every one of them, from the oldest to the youngest!"

The best mirror is an old friend. —PROVERB

CYNTHIA TELLS A STORY about how her friend Debra helped her learn to be a more compassionate friend:

"I came from an okay family life. My parents took good care of me, but as a family we weren't very adept at talking about emotional issues.

"So when I grew up, my sense of compassion wasn't as well developed as it should have been. In retrospect, I think I can say that I probably wasn't the best friend or lover that I could have been, just because I never learned how to listen when necessary.

"But my friend Debra helped me change that. When we met at work, I had been encountering some personal problems that at times seemed overwhelming. She would sit for hours and listen to me talk through my problems. I really appreciated her ability to listen. I felt loved and cared about because my feelings were important to someone else.

"Today, when my friends have problems I try to be a friend like Debra was to me. I think she taught me to be a better listener. Her example has helped my friends, and it has the added benefit of making me a better person."

I Can Always Count On You

To paraphrase Woody Allen, a great part of success in life is merely "showing up." So it is with friendship. Sometimes a great friend is the one who always manages to be there to support you in the times when you need it. And sometimes "showing up" requires a bit more action, as illustrated by the letter Donna wrote us, opposite. We would like you to share a time when your friend has shown up for you—whatever that has meant to you.

You were truly there for me when . . .

AS ELISE SAYS OF HER FRIEND KYM, "She's really a show-upper. I'd be having a party and she maybe was not feeling that great, but she would always come for a little while. I think that's kind of an amazing thing. To have friends who really show up, on whom you can rely."

Donna shared this story with us, "Two years ago, when my two young sons were only three years old and seven months of age, respectively, I was diagnosed with breast cancer. Within the next two weeks, five of my oldest friends organized our baby-sitting, house cleaning, errands and meals. The most amazing of these was the meal preparation. Each of the women chose a night to cook dinner. A red cooler was placed outside my back door and every evening (Monday through Friday), a meal was left inside the cooler. Occasionally, a nice card was left for my husband and me. This continued for six months—the length of my chemotherapy. It was fun wondering what surprise or delicacy was waiting in the cooler, as well as to guess and joke about the culinary talents of each of my friends. When I finished chemotherapy, my friends wanted to continue bringing the daily meals but I insisted that they had done enough (they all worked and had their own families). My husband and I made awards for each of them which described their personal culinary talents (or lack thereof) and we all had lots of laughs. I also gave each woman a plant as a symbol of hope, renewal, sustenance and new growth—something they had been giving me for the previous six months. These female friends are very dear to me and I love them immensely—I don't know how I would have survived the ordeal without them."

We Had the Best Time

Women told us that their friends were those with whom they enjoyed themselves—having a raucous time or simply experiencing some tranquillity together. We invite you to remember an enjoyable experience you have had with your friend.

I really enjoyed it when we . . .

As one woman described her friend, "One companionable Saturday when we'd been reading silently for several hours, Karen looked up and commented, 'You know, being with you is like being by myself.' It was one of the highest compliments about a friendship that I have ever received."

Holly had this story about her friend and their shared stage experience: "Susan and I worked together as YMCA day-camp counselors. We always did skits and songs together. The kids loved us because we were such goofs. One time we decided to act out this silly song about a farm couple's rooster. I played the farmer and she was the farmer's wife *and* the rooster. The song was totally stupid, downright funny, and we just couldn't get through it without laughing. We kept practicing but would start cracking up. When we got in front of the whole camp it wasn't any better. We were actually lying on the floor, howling. I don't think we ever got through it. The kids thought we were a hoot and repeatedly asked for an encore throughout the rest of the summer."

Wild Women

With the strength of a friend bolstering us, we can make trouble or be rebellious in ways that we never would have alone. Whether it is poking fun at someone (who desperately deserves it) in order to maintain a sense of humor in a difficult situation, marching to stand up for a cause in which we believe, or sidestepping some regulations to accomplish a necessary objective, women need to stir up matters. We think that women have forgotten in the last few years that we have more strength in numbers, but we see it proven over and over again when we are with our girlfriends. Please share a time when you and your friend or friends have made some trouble.

You and I stirred things up when we . . .

Things Only You Understand

"I wish you could have been there."
When our friendship develops with
another woman, we experience more
and more instances when we wish our
friend could have been by our side for
moral support or merely to share the
pleasure or humor of an event. A friend's
knowledge of you enables her to under-
stand fully a situation's significance to
you. As Dorothy, a seventy-five-year-old
woman, writes of Janet, her friend of
seventy-three years: "It has been such
a part of my life to have had a girlfriend
like Janet. She understands me better
than anyone." When our friend is not
with us, we often make a point of
relating the story to her later to hear
what she thinks of the situation. Can you
think of a time when you have wished
your friend was with you to share your
experience?

I missed you most when . . .

The Agony and the Ecstasy

Girlfriends are not just women with whom we have fun. A friendship varied in its history, peppered with conflict as well as accord, is one that becomes more and more valuable. As we go through difficult times as well as enjoyable ones, we create rich layers of experience that test and ultimately strengthen the friendship. What results is a lush tapestry of memories shared with your friend. Record some of the highs and the lows of your friendship here.

The worst advice you ever gave me was . . .

The person I least liked that you were romantically involved with was . . .

The worst thing you ever made me do was . . .

THE WORST PICTURE OF
THE TWO OF US

THE BEST PICTURE OF
THE TWO OF US

The best advice you ever gave me was . . .

The best gift you ever gave me was . . .

*The person whom I most approved of
in your romantic life . . .*

The best compliment you ever gave me was . . .

The Strangest Thing Happened to Us

There are those times that are not funny in the "ha-ha" sense, but funny in the *strange* sense, and neither you nor your friend is ever able to figure out what happened or explain why. We are always relieved to have our friend there with us in those moments for many reasons, not the least of which is to assure us that we are not losing our mind; our friend experienced it, too.

The strangest thing that ever happened to us was . . .

WHEN CHRISTINA AND HANNA WERE TRAVELING TOGETHER IN EUROPE, they found that, for some bizarre reason, Hanna was under the constant scrutiny of the police. Christina recounts: "We started noticing it when we flew from London to Paris, and the customs people were especially diligent in going through Hanna's bags. They pulled out her socks, unrolled them, and went carefully through her cosmetic bag. Then they drew Hanna aside and did a very thorough once-over with the hand-held metal detector. It was embarrassing, but we decided it was just a fluke. But throughout the trip we had 'official eyes' on us, which finally culminated in the south of France."

Hanna continued, "We had just left a rather remote tourist site and were walking back to our car. All of a sudden, a police car filled with five policemen, sirens wailing, pulled up behind our car. They were definitely looking for *us*. They demanded all of our papers and started firing questions at me in French. I struggled to remember how to say '1960' in French—my year of birth—after I finally figured out that they were questioning me as to my knowledge of the documents. Luckily, I had a horrible cold, so I couldn't really muster up fear at that point. After about half an hour, they either took pity on me or gave up. Perhaps I met some description of a fugitive, or perhaps we were providing amusement on a hot summer day. We will never know what happened, but it was *very* strange. We still talk about that trip."

Our Rites of Passage

Friendship becomes stronger the more rites of passage we survive together — experiences so common in the lives of girls and women that they mark our shared growth. The more memories and transitions we share with our friends, the deeper and more complex the relationships. How many of these transforming experiences you have shared with your friend will depend on when you met her, but rites of passage continue throughout life. They can be enjoyable or ones we would choose never to live through again. In fact, sometimes distressing situations can bind us together more than pleasant memories. We have listed a few common rites of womanhood opposite, and we encourage you to record your own rites of passage you endured with your friend.

Some of the rites of passage that we have experienced together are . . .

True friendship is never serene. –MARIE DE SÉVIGNÉ

Girl Scouts/Campfire Girls • First periods • Gym suits • Eccentric teachers • Sports tryouts • First Kisses • High school proms • Graduations • College freshman orientations • Exams • Late night popcorn • Fixing each other up on blind dates • Trading clothes • Sharing secrets • Being bridesmaids • Job interviews • First jobs • Getting lost on vacation together • Having to be honest about something difficult •

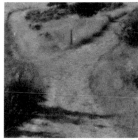

Disapproving of each other's mates • Trying out new recipes on each other • Receiving a promotion • Being fired • Children • Arguments • Getting divorced • Adopting a pet • Losing or gaining weight (or neither) • Being attracted to the same person • Recovering from an addiction • Leaving a job to pursue a dream • Ending a

bad relationship • Improving a good relationship • Death of a parent • First gray hair • Menopause • New Beliefs • Grandchildren • Retirement

You Had to Be There

Sometimes you and your friend or friends find yourselves in a situation that seems stunningly hilarious. Unfortunately, when trying to describe it to someone else, you receive nothing but a blank stare and perhaps a polite chuckle. Then, magically, when you revisit the scene with your girlfriend, you find yourselves doubled over in laughter once again. These, of course, are the "you had to be there" moments. We invite you to share the stories that you and your friend carry with you—moments that can come back to you and your friend in an instant but that you can never succeed in explaining to anyone else.

We always laugh when we remember . . .

Every day, and the living of it, has to be a conscious creation in which discipline and order are relieved with some play and pure foolishness. —MAY SARTON

SHARON STILL LAUGHS WHEN SHE TELLS THIS STORY: "My relationship with my friend Laura has always been a humorous one. We're always doing bizarre things and getting caught in weird situations. One summer my friends and I were camping near San Diego. We decided to go skinny-dipping. Afterward, when we were putting our clothes back on, I realized I couldn't find my bra. Laura and I looked everywhere, but it was nowhere to be found. But I couldn't go on the rest of the trip without a bra! Finally, Laura turned around while I was facing her, and I saw that my bra was latched onto her hair. The hook had gotten caught, somehow, on her curly locks. I couldn't stop laughing. We had spent all that time looking, when all along my bra was hanging from her head!"

You Really Helped Me With My Family

Every woman has problems to work out with her family, whether with her spouse, mate, children, parents, brothers, or sisters. These can be life-changing events, as when a parent becomes terminally ill, or more everyday events, such as a running disagreement with a child about keeping his or her room clean. Sometimes our emotional ties with family members obscure our problem-solving skills. We myopically grasp for a solution when we cannot even see the issue clearly. At these times, a friend can step in and state the issue and maybe even suggest a few approaches to the problem—actions you would have been able to suggest if the situation didn't involve your family. Frequently women told us that their friends were able to help them get through a confusing or difficult situation with their families or through the loneliness of losing a family member or even not having a family at all. Sometimes friends just step in when you need a break. We invite you to record a time when your friend has helped with a family issue.

You really helped me with my family when . . .

ELLEN AND HER FIVE FRIENDS BLOW OFF SOME STEAM when they gather together every year. Among their other activities, they crown with a tiara the woman who has the best (or worst) story about her family. As Ellen says, "It's great therapy and lots of laughs! It's the one time a year we can be ourselves — not somebody's mom or wife."

GAIL AND MYRA MET IN THE SEVENTH GRADE. Myra's father had been dead for eight years, and she was being raised by a mother who was having her own problems: "Almost every other year my mom would spend four to six months committed to a state hospital. I always felt ashamed, lonely, and afraid. After meeting Gail, I discovered that a friend can help you to feel okay. She always invited me to her house, and she never asked questions about my home.

"When I turned sixteen, and again my mom was hospitalized, I wanted to visit her. The state hospital was a scary place — bars on the doors and windows, keys to get onto the ward, and the people, so sad, so sick, and all the yelling. Without being asked, Gail traveled with me on the three buses that it took to get to the hospital. Right then I knew I had a friend for life. I knew that Gail didn't go with me because she was curious or eager to see an 'insane asylum.' She went because I needed my friend to be with me. I needed to not be alone. And I needed to not be ashamed." Gail and Myra have been friends for thirty years.

A Very Happy Birthday

Women told us that one of their favorite ways to celebrate a friendship was to make a friend's birthday one to remember. Many women feel embarrassed to be the focus of attention yet feel grateful when friends show they are important enough to make a fuss over. And who else but a close friend knows what a woman would enjoy for her birthday celebration? We would like to encourage you to record a birthday celebration (either for your birthday or your friend's birthday) that was memorable for you. You may want to include an idea of how you would like to celebrate your birthday or a friend's birthday in the future.

My favorite birthday celebration with you was. . .

We are always the same age inside. —GERTRUDE STEIN

It is sad to grow old but nice to ripen. — BRIGITTE BARDOT

ELISE TELLS THIS STORY of when a certain birthday gift was particularly important: "In the space of a month, I had started working for a company that had not been my first choice, my boyfriend was leaving to move to Hawaii for a couple of months, and my best friend and roommate was moving out to live with her boyfriend. Both my boyfriend and my roommate were leaving on April 1, and my thirtieth birthday was on March 29. I was feeling abandoned and lonely. On my birthday I got this huge bouquet of tulips from Leslie, and the card said, 'I'll always be here for you.' And I still have that card, which I look at all the time, because, the thing is, it's really true. She really, really is always there. I have another card at home that just says, 'I love you, Leslie.' We actually always send each other flowers on our birthdays. But that was the beginning of that tradition. That was the first card I got from her. It was just so needed, and when I see it, I know I still need it."

Now We Can Look Back and Laugh

We have all been in physical circumstances and emotional situations with
our friends that we took very seriously at
the time but with the passing of time or
more maturity (or both) came to seem
trivial or (if enough time passed) even
funny. Remember the surprise of the
disastrous home perm you gave each
other? the anxious waiting for your
annual review at the office? the agony
of the oral exam you both had to take?
the time you wanted to wring her neck?
the suffocatingly boring (or shockingly
enjoyable) New Year's Eve party? What
are some of your favorite "remember
whens" that you and your friend share?

Remember when
we experimented with . . .

we got dressed up for . . .

we were both stressed out about . . .

we celebrated because . . .

we were so annoyed that . . .

HELEN TELLS THIS STORY of her best friend's a-little-too-honest approach:
"Pat had been married for a number of years when I met my future husband.
One week after we started dating, I took him to meet Pat and her husband because
I knew she'd tell him how wonderful I was, right? After I had introduced him to
her husband, Pat came in from the kitchen (looking like Donna Reed) and, wiping
flour from her hands onto her apron, took his arm and almost immediately blurted
out all of my embarrassing moments: 'Come into the kitchen with me while I tell
you about Helen. Did you know she gets corn up her nose when she eats corn on
the cob? Did she ever tell you about the time she peed in the elevator?' That's
honesty for you!" Somehow Helen and Pat are still friends, and neither will forget
that moment! Neither, of course, will Helen's husband of now thirty-five years!

A Day to Remember

The day was important . . . but having
a friend there makes it even more
memorable. On these occasions, we would
enjoy ourselves anyway, but with her
there, we laugh a bit more loudly, breathe
a bit more deeply, and feel a bit more at
ease. What landmark day was made more
wonderful because your girlfriend was
there to share it with you?

*You helped me make a
special day better by . . .*

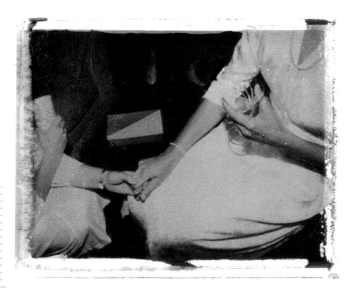

KATHLEEN TELLS OF SHOPPING FOR HER WEDDING DRESS with her friend of thirty-six years. "Mary is sophisticated, with dramatic looks and lots of confidence when dealing with salespeople. I feel most comfortable in black jeans and a cotton sweater and prefer to cruise stores anonymously. I looked forward to our shopping trip with some trepidation. At our first stop, Mary's favorite boutique, she was talking to the sales help and the owner like old friends as I walked to the back rack, picked up a moss-green silk dress, and held it up to my face. It was the same color as my eyes. A tiny saleswoman appeared and invited me to try it on. I declined, knowing it would never fit my budget or my ample hips. Mary walked over and firmly encouraged me. Sure enough, the dress transformed me into an elegant bride. She then surprised me by buying it as her wedding gift to me! On my wedding day I felt and looked beautiful. Mary sat near the front of the chapel, and we shared a wonderful smile as I walked down the aisle."

THE BIG DAY

You probably have a favorite photo, some dried flowers or other
mementos, that remind you of a big day in your life.
Please attach them here.

Thanks For The Nudge

There comes a time in every woman's life when she stands uncertainly facing a crossroads. At times like these, friends prove their mettle. We have all bared our souls and shown the ugly doubts we have about ourselves to our friends. They not only can hear our secrets and still accept us and love us, but they also can help us make choices that are healthy for us. Many women we interviewed told us that their women friends helped them make a crucial decision, urged them to try something new, or pointed them in the right direction. Has your girlfriend given you needed insight or help at just the right moment?

You gave me a push in the right direction when you . . .

Oh, the comfort, the inexpressible comfort of feeling safe with a person, having neither to weigh thoughts nor measure words, but pouring them all right out, just as they are, chaff and grain together; certain that a faithful hand will take and sift them, keep what is worth keeping, and then with the breath of kindness blow the rest away. —DINAH MARIA MULOCK CRAIK

MICHELLE AND TINA MET IN THE 1950s when they were both young women working as nurses in New York City. They began sharing an apartment when each of their room-mates, who worked nights, realized that they could economize by all living together. But it was a few years later that their friendship really took off. Tina had relocated to San Francisco, and when Michelle moved there, she looked up her ex-roomie. In the new city, the two became good friends. Michelle remembers, "We were there for each other. She is someone I can call in the middle of the night." The two young women had endless conversations about every topic under the sun.

A subject they often returned to was Michelle's problem with alcohol. Tina confessed that her friend's drinking worried her and that she wanted to help. They came up with ideas and plans to solve the problem, but these solutions never worked for very long. Finally, one spring day, Tina suggested contacting the National Council on Alcoholism. She offered to call for her friend, but Michelle decided to make the call herself. She did, got into a treatment program, and began attending Twelve-Step meetings. She has been sober now for twenty-one years. Every year around the first of April the two friends take each other out for breakfast, each year to a different place, to celebrate Michelle's sobriety and that turning point in their friendship. Looking back at that fateful day, Michelle remembers, "I trusted it was the right thing to do if my friend said that it was."

I Was So Proud of You

We share our secret dreams and our saddest disappointments with our girl-friends. Only they know how hard it is to confront a co-worker, start a new career, leave an unhealthy relationship, or grieve the loss of a love. It takes great courage to face both success and loss. Our girlfriends are those who stand with us proudly after we have made a tough decision or realized a long-held dream. What has been the most impressive moment of your girlfriend's life? When were you proudest of her?

I was proudest of you when . . .

ELENA SHARED HER STORY WITH US ABOUT HER FRIEND LINDA: "For years Linda had been in a difficult marriage, one in which she had been emotionally manipulated by her husband. He constantly professed his desire to change in order to make the relationship work, but he used any dialogue between them to find fault with Linda and bully her into accommodating to all his rules. She tried to make it work for years, but I watched the vitality drain out of her as she tried to adjust to an ever-changing set of conditions for the relationship. Finally, she faced the truth that nothing was ever going to change, and she left. I think it was probably one of the most difficult, yet necessary, things she has ever had to do. I was so proud of her when she finally said 'no more.' "

WEEK AFTER WEEK, LAURA AND TAMARA met in a pub after work and planned how they would each escape their jobs. After years of scheming, brainstorming, weeping, and hoping, Laura took the risk of leaving her job to pursue her dream of producing theater. The first play she produced made it to Broadway and was nominated for a Tony award! Thrilled for her friend, Tamara attended the opening and recalls, "I was so proud of Laura. There she was, looking cool as a cucumber, talking with all those celebrities as if she had been attending opening nights for the past twenty years. It's hard to put into words how proud I was of her. I knew how far she had come, so I was all the more excited for her good fortune."

Photo Opportunities

Please include on this page any photos or mementos
that you have been saving from your early friendship.

Nothing Like The Present

Each contact with a human being is so rare,
so precious, one should preserve it.

—ANAÏS NIN

We Are The Same...

We can feel so close to our girlfriends that it may be hard to tell us apart. Often similar interests, attitudes, and opinions draw us close to each other. How are you and your girlfriend alike?

We are similar in that we both . . .

There is space within sisterhood for likeness and difference, for the subtle differences that challenge and delight; there is space for disappointment—and surprise. —CHRISTINE DOWNING

...But Different

Ever try to put two like-charged sides of magnets together? They push against each other. But turn one around, and smack! The two magnets snap together with a powerful pull. Girlfriends can be like magnets, drawn to each other not by similarities but by differences. Perhaps there is some aspect of her that you admire, or perhaps those differences just intrigue you. How are you different?

MARY LOUISE AND HELEN always knew how different they were. From the moment they became friends in fifth grade they compared themselves to the characters in the fairy tale "Snow White and Rose Red." Mary Louise's hair was shiny, black, and long, she was a talented musician, and she traveled extensively with her large family. Conversely, Helen had short, curly, light brown hair. She wrote poetry and read fairy tales in the neat garden of the tiny house where her family lived for forty-five years.

Their differing styles—Mary Louise intense and impulsive, Helen quiet and introspective—are reflected in many of their life choices. As their friendship approaches its fourth decade, the two continue to marvel at and cherish the distinct perspectives they bring to each other's lives.

WE ARE DIFFERENT IN THAT

I am	while you are
I like	while you like
I eat	while you eat
I wear	while you wear
I drink	while you drink
I believe	while you believe
I hate	while you hate
I love	while you love

I Know You Are Committed To Me

Ever wonder why your friendship lasts through the good and the bad, the ups and the downs? Like an enduring marriage, the bond between women friends survives life's struggles through sturdy commitment. That commitment has important consequences for each of the friends, a knowledge that someone is always on your side, a constancy on which you can call at any time. How does commitment show itself in your relationship?

When a friend asks, there is no tomorrow. — PROVERB

I know that we are committed to our friendship because . . .

CARMEN MET CATHY in the late seventies when they both worked as weekend house-parents at a children's home. For the two years that they worked together, they spent every Saturday night talking after the children had gone to bed. When they moved on to other jobs, Carmen and Cathy decided to continue their weekly meetings and have done so to this day.

Recalling one year in particular, Carmen comments, "Cathy's father died suddenly and I lost a very significant romantic relationship. We were both shell-shocked by our losses. Even though we weren't much company, we kept meeting every week. Just having Cathy show up week after week meant so much. About a year later, when we were in a bit better shape, Cathy looked over at me and said, 'Hey, I remember you.' We laughed, and I realized that I didn't have to be in good shape to be loved by her."

You Are Like Family To Me

Women sometimes bond so tightly that each of them becomes an addition to their respective families. From being included in holiday dinners and family vacations to participating in difficult family issues, many women are considered part of the families of their friends. In other situations, our women friends become our "families away from home" if we are too far away to see our families on a regular basis. And sometimes they are the ones who become our spiritual families — people to whom, for whatever reason, we feel more comfortable going with our confessions, problems, and achievements. These women may be the first people with whom we "feel at home." Many different circumstances and connections have prompted women to describe their girlfriends as "like family" or "the sister I always wanted." How does your girlfriend "feel like family?"

You feel like part of my family because . . .

There's a kind of emotional exploration you plumb with a friend that you don't really do with your family. —BETTE MIDLER

IN AN EARLIER TIME, women may have gone to a favorite aunt or grandmother to discuss a family issue. Now many times we go to those women friends who can, like an honored relative, be trusted to listen and show discretion with a delicate family problem, and who we know look at us and our families through eyes of affection. When we spoke with Betty and Sara, they described coaching each other in their respective marital relationships. Betty talks about the effects of that coaching: "I probably will get to stay married to this man for the rest of my life. A few years ago, when Jeff and I weren't having such a good time, Sara said, 'You're not leaving him. I'll nail your shoes to the floor.' "

Sara interrupted to remind her gently, "No, it was your *feet* I threatened to nail to the floor. You can walk out of your shoes."

Betty, remembering, nodded in agreement. "I think about that image all the time. We want each other's relationships to work."

Like a trusted family member, Betty and Sara can rely on one another to tell the truth, while keeping each other's best interests constantly in view.

That's Just The Way We Are

When you get together with your girlfriend, do you remind yourselves of characters you've seen in the movies? Do your adventures deserve titles from epic novels? Or maybe the two of you are best compared to characters from a situation comedy! Have some fun by sitting down with your girlfriend and finding out which of the following describes your friendship. Feel free to add your own titles or names!

THE TELEVISION SHOW THAT BEST DESCRIBES OUR FRIENDSHIP IS:

- [ ] *The Young and the Restless*
- [ ] *Gladiators*
- [ ] *To Tell the Truth*
- [ ] *The Bold and the Beautiful*
- [ ] *Designing Women*
- [ ] *Star Trek: Voyager*

THE GIRLFRIEND DUO THAT BEST EXEMPLIFIES OUR FRIENDSHIP IS:

- [ ] **Lucy and Ethel**
- [ ] **Ruth and Naomi**
- [ ] **Thelma and Louise**
- [ ] **Cybill and Marianne**
- [ ] **Diane and Fergie**
- [ ] **Cagney and Lacey**

THE BOOK TITLE THAT BEST DESCRIBES OUR ADVENTURES TOGETHER IS:

- [ ] *Pride and Prejudice*
- [ ] *Sense and Sensibility*
- [ ] *The Agony and the Ecstasy*
- [ ] *Gone with the Wind*
- [ ] *Two Serious Ladies*

We have left some space here for you to attach items that are typical of the activities you and your friend enjoy together. These items could include yarn, postcards, bookmarks, leaves, recipes, swizzle sticks, or matchbook covers—whatever reminds you of you and your friend! If your shared hobby is too big or messy to put on the page (like ballooning or eating pasta), draw a sketch, put together a collage or add photos.

How Did You Know That?

Many women told us that as their friendships grew closer, one or both friends would start "knowing" things about the other without being told. From understanding each other so well that they finished each other's sentences to actually feeling that a friend was in trouble with no other indication that that was so, many women said their intuition was sharpened with a close friend. Can you think of a time when you have had some intuitive knowledge about your friend, or vice versa?

There's something so beautiful in coming on one's very own inmost thoughts in another. In one way it's one of the greatest pleasures one has. —OLIVE SCHREINER

I (You) just knew, without being told, that . . .

BARBARA AND LENA have had a strong, almost magical connection since
they first met in 1975 in the Swiss Alps. Years later, unbeknownst to
Barbara, Lena was undergoing surgery to remove a cyst on her thyroid.
That night, Barbara had a dream that Lena had been cut on her neck.
Alarmed, she called her friend the next morning, only to find out that
Lena's incision was at the same place on her body that Barbara had seen
in her dream. Lena realized that the bond between her and Barbara
was stronger and more significant than she'd previously thought. And
she promised to tell Barbara the next time she had surgery (since she
apparently couldn't keep it from her anyway!).

Did I Ever Tell You About Her?

Having a close woman friend is wonderful even when you aren't together because you can tell others about her when she's not around! Of all the stories you've told other people about your girlfriend, which one is your very favorite?

My favorite story I tell other people about you is . . .

JULIE TELLS HER FAVORITE STORY ABOUT MEETING HER FRIEND CHERYL: "When I was twelve, my mother got the bright idea that she, my fourteen-year-old brother, and I would spend the summers at a lake cottage together. By June I desperately missed my friends and was bored out of my mind.

"Then, one day, a miracle occurred. I looked out the window, and there were people on our dock silhouetted against the sun. And they were kids! One was my brother, another was a teenage boy, and then I saw *her*.

"She was tall, lean, very tanned, and clad in the most exotic fake leopardskin bathing suit I had ever seen. I don't think I have ever been more happy to see someone in my life. From that moment on we were best friends. We spent every summer together at 'the lake' until we graduated from high school. During the winter months we wrote letters, sent pictures and kooky tapes of conversation, and other stuff.

"Today, thirty years later, we are still close friends. Although we now live two thousand miles apart and rarely get together anymore, the minute we hear each other on the telephone we are immediately catapulted back into our valued friendship. To this day, when I hear her voice, I recall that little girl in an exotic leopardskin bathing suit who saved me from a summer of boredom."

A Few of Our Favorite Things...

Sometimes we like the same things, sometimes we don't. How do you and your girlfriend compare on your preferences and opinions?

	MY FAVORITE	*YOUR FAVORITE*
Talk show		
Romantic comedy		
Leading man		
Leading woman		
Color		
Late-night snack		
Type of mate		
Vacation spot		
Lingerie		
Musician		
Pet		
Junk food		
Flower		

She knows my heart and my mind, how I react to certain situations. And I know the same about her. —HOLLY TAINES

And A Few We Both Disdain

Don't expect girlfriends to be "sugar and spice and everything nice"! No way. One of the pleasures of being girlfriends is putting our noses in the air—together. What do you and your girlfriend mutually abhor and reject with glee?

WE SHARE A MUTUAL DISLIKE FOR . . .

Men who wear

Saleswomen who say

Movies about

Underwear that

Mothers who

Friends who ask

Hairdressers who suggest

Bosses who say

Drivers who

Fathers who

Party-goers who

Politicians who

Our Time

A shared cup of tea every Tuesday
morning after the kids are off to school,
a few minutes together in each other's
offices over a soda, pasta and movies
every Thursday night, a hike or a poetry
reading once a month, even an annual
reunion especially planned to review
the previous year of your lives and plan
the future: These are remembered
traditions that honor a friendship. Place
your remembrances here and write a
brief description of why these shared
moments are so valuable to you.

For "our time" together, we . . .

"Stay" is a charming word in a friend's vocabulary. —LOUISA MAY ALCOTT

SOME FRIENDSHIP RITUALS grow out of wonderful coincidence. Twelve years ago, Marilyn and five of her acquaintances became pregnant at about the same time. The six new mothers met weekly for what they laughingly called "baby lunch." The babies would play together until their nap time, when the women would prepare an elaborate lunch for themselves. Marilyn emphasizes that it was definitely not potluck. She remembers eating borscht from beets grown in her garden and apple pie made from scratch. One summer day all six toddlers, dressed in diapers, were photographed sitting side by side in a doorway. A few years later, one of the moms noticed that the kids were sitting in the doorway again. Out came a camera, and a tradition was born. The children, now rangy preteens, are one another's best friends, and their mothers still love sharing meals and conversation. They meet for monthly dinners, without their kids, at various Indian restaurants in their university town in Connecticut. "Baby lunch" has become "Ladies Night Out." The friendships endure.

Photo Opportunities

Friends are gardeners in the garden that is me. —CATHERINE S. SMITH

Looking Forward

. . . Old friends, we swim our slow, unathletic laps.
We were intense, emotional girls. We believed
that art made life worth living, and it does.
We thought that life would give us everything, and it has.
We are still burning, plunging through the pool's bright surface,
buoyant in the sweet and bitter water.

— FROM "SWIMMING, FOR MARILYN," CAROLYN MILLER

As We Grow Older

Imagine the future. Our friends will be carrying with them all we've shared with them—our secrets, our dreams, our best and worst moments. What do you see when you see yourself and your friend together many years from now? Will your relationship be different? Will it be the same? What do you want your girlfriend to remind you about in the years to come? Perhaps you want her to remind you to take that painting class you've always wanted to take or to travel to New Zealand like you've been hoping to all these years or to sit side by side watching the waves lap on the shore. Perhaps you need her to remind you to keep your mind curious or your sense of humor well oiled. We invite you to use your imagination to picture you and your friend in the future.

As we grow older, our relationship will be different in that . . .

Our relationship will be the same in that . . .

These are the things I want you to remind me of as I grow older:

These are the things that I want you to prevent me from doing:

JULIE TELLS THIS STORY ABOUT HER LIFELONG FRIEND: "Connie and I have been friends since we were both five years old. We've been through it all together—kindergarten, grammar school, high school, college, job hunting, marriages—you name it, we've done it. Today we are in our early forties. I am unmarried, living alone. Connie is married with a brand new baby. When I recently met the baby, I was overcome with emotion as I watched Connie feed her daughter. I realized that with the birth of her child, a whole new identity had emerged in my friend of so many years. Like all people, she gets more and more complex, more and more interesting, more and more deep as she grows older and takes on more roles.

"That day represented much more than a casual visit; it was another passage in our eternally entwined lives. No matter how well I think we know each other, my friend and I will continually be developing new aspects of ourselves. Each new side will be a discovery, fresh and exciting. I am looking forward to watching the new aspects of our personalities develop as we live out our lives as friends."

Our Future Adventures

Some of your dreams of the future would not be complete without your friend being there to share them with you. What adventures would you like to have with your girlfriend when you are both old women? Some dreams are possible, others are adventures of imagination. Record the adventures in your mind that you and your friend could share if you pulled out all the stops!

If the two of us ran away from home for one month together, we would (please check all that apply):

☐ Drive a dogsled across Alaska

☐ Ride the Orient Express from Paris to Constantinople

☐ Blow our wad in Monte Carlo

☐ Drive cross-country in a pink Cadillac convertible

☐ Cruise the Caribbean on a private yacht (with a crew of young, swarthy seamen)

☐ Hide out in a cabin by a lake

☐ Ski the slopes of Switzerland

☐ Travel the Australian Outback in a jeep

☐ Go on an African photo safari

☐ Search for a guru in the Himalayas

☐ Lose ourselves in the Mall of America

As we grow older, I'd like to do these
things with you:

Betsy and I always say we're going to live in the south of France
and have yappy dogs and cute houseboys. —TAMARA TRAEDER

I Trust You

No one wants to think about endings, and perhaps death is a subject we'd like to avoid. But one day, we all have to say good-bye. Our close friends can carry on for us after we are gone by caring for our loved ones, safeguarding treasured possessions, or supporting causes to which we were devoted. Knowing that someone will take care of things after we are gone can make living today a bit more comforting. What would you entrust to your friend's care if you were gone?

If something ever happened to me,
I'd trust you to . . .

ONE WOMAN TOLD THIS STORY: "My dear friend and I have made a pact with each other in the event that something should happen to either of us. I have promised to adopt her cat because she trusts me to take care of it the way she would. If something should happen to me and I was unable to take care of myself, she has promised me that she would immediately come to my home and destroy all my journals that I have kept throughout the years. Many of the journals were written when I was going through a very angry period in my life, and I am afraid they would cause a lot of pain if they were revealed. I suppose I should just get rid of them, but they are such an important part of me that I cannot bring myself to do so yet. However, I rest easy knowing that she would get rid of them for me and save others from the angst of reading them. I have even told her she can read them if she's curious. I don't think there is anything in there she doesn't already know."

What I Wish For You

Sometimes our friends can see what
we most need and can make wishes
for us that we somehow cannot bring
ourselves to make. We asked several
women what they would wish for their
closest friend and have included a list of
their responses on the opposite page.
What good things do you want for your
friend in the coming years?

My wish for you this year is . . .

For future years I wish for you . . .

Here are some wishes women made for their respective closest friend:

I wish for her . . .

" . . . the courage to make the changes in her life that she needs to make."

" . . . a wonderful relationship with someone who makes her feel good about herself."

" . . . peace of mind and help to get the time to do what she needs to do in life."

" . . . self-confidence."

" . . . some time just for herself."

" . . . a solid chocolate Easter bunny every Easter, a great relationship with someone who loves her, and the means to get what she wants out of life." (Okay, that was three wishes, but that's acceptable.)

" . . . the ability to relax and enjoy her talents and prosperity."

" . . . to be with someone — for her to share her wonderful home with a loving husband."

" . . . a life of artmaking, filled with love and respect."

Celebrations

We frequently use birthdays as a means of showing our appreciation for a friend. But sometimes it is appropriate to recognize the friendship as well as the friend. When we take time out to recognize and celebrate an important friendship, both parties feel appreciated and the relationship is strengthened. Various anniversaries are celebrated in romantic relationships to turn our hearts and minds toward that connection; memories are triggered and the present bond is reinforced. What do women do to acknowledge the central role their friendships play in their lives? All kinds of things—from walking down memory lane to a formal recognition of your relationship.

We invite you to record here a way you have celebrated your friendship or a ritual you would like to share with your friend. How would you like to commemorate your friendship?

ROSE AND MARCIA DEVELOPED A FRIENDSHIP RITUAL on a trip that they made together. In their room at a New England bed-and-breakfast, they lit candles and incense to set the mood. The women sat face-to-face and told each other what their friendship meant to them. They exchanged small gifts as they often did when getting together. One gift stood out and became the focal point for future rituals. It was a piece of polished rose quartz from Marcia to Rose. Since then the women bring the pink stone along when they meet, and they take turns keeping it. They exchange it hand-to-hand at some point during their visit. It has become a symbol of their love and friendship.

WHEN MARY AND KATHLEEN WERE IN PITTSBURGH to attend the reunion of their Catholic high school, they drove by the parish complex. On impulse they walked around the playground between the yellow brick church and school and recognized Eddie, still working as the janitor. To their surprise, he remembered them, and let them into the choir loft where they had spent many mornings of their girlhood. As they walked up the narrow, dark spiral staircase behind Eddie, memories flooded back. Mary had played the organ and sung weekday masses and funerals at the church. Kathleen was her page turner. The friends recalled stifling their giggles during quiet services and eating the coconut crullers smuggled in from Smoody's bakery. Mostly they remembered being so young and close. The short visit to this private place helped them retrieve priceless memories that had been lost over the years.

Saving Room For You

We have left this page blank so that you have space to record future events together. Enjoy!